# The Energy Behind the Word

**Prophet Hiddekel Jephte Katemo**

Copyright@2021 by Hiddekel Katemo Jephte

This book may not be reproduced in any form either by print, photocopy, recording, or any other means without written permission from the author.

Permission will only be granted on request. The use of short quotations or occasional page copying for personal use or group study is permitted and encouraged. All scriptures are quoted from the King James Version, Amplified Version and the NIV.

# DEDICATION

This book is dedicated to all humanity, to the Holy Ghost Kingdom Ministries International family. I thank God the Father for the privilege to let His Spirit teach me this book and for revealing this mystery to us.

I encountered God at age 11 and in 2008 the calling of God upon my life began to manifest.

In 2013, I encountered a vision, it was 5am in the morning, while I was a permanent worker in one of the mining companies.

My shift changed every 15 days starting from 3pm till the next day, and in the morning from 7am to 3pm. During one of my evening shifts, I went to the mountain as it was my habit to have morning prayers from 5am until 12pm.

When I left the mountain, I returned home to prepare for work. On getting home, I was so tired that I decided to rest. While resting, my eyes opened, I found myself in front of the tabernacle of Moses. Curiously, when I looked inside the door,

I saw a man sitting on a throne with a long white beards but I could not see the face only the beards and crown, and He asked me to come in.

When I took the first step, I realised I was in front of Him and He told me to kneel, which I did. Then He took anointing oil, poured it on me and told me to go. When I stood, I noticed there was a person beside me, when I checked it was Aaron and Moses.

After I left the tabernacle, I found myself in a big hall preaching to empty chairs but holding a hammer as a microphone.
It took a while to understand this vision, up until I started serving, I was doubting if I was indeed called by Elohim.

After my night prayer session, the Lord opened my eyes again and I saw many people in a very dark place and they didn't know how to get out of it, then I saw a big board with a verse from exodus

rising from above, I heard a voice speaking to me about the mission Yahweh gave me and the significances of the hammer I was holding as a microphone. This book is from my encounter years ago. I have a lot written in this book, it took me 3 years to write this book and I understand why the enemy didn't want this book to be released.
Enjoy Reading!!

# TABLE OF CONTENT

INTRODUCTION

THE WORD OF MAN AND THE WORD OF GOD

WORD AND TIME

THE ENERGY

THE ETERNAL LIFE IS THE WORD OF GOD

THE AUTHORITY OF A MAN

HOW TO BENEFIT FROM THE WORD OF GOD

HOW TO IMPACT WITH YOUR WORD

THE POWER OF YOUR TONGUE

THE WORDS OF PARENTS

WORDS AND MOUTH

WE ARE GODS

# INTRODUCTION

The word is the power of command which God has placed for His creation. The reason why God is not punishing the world, Satan and men who do not obey Him is because of His word. Since He placed his word ahead of Him to rule and command, as a true model He does not act beyond His word. There is a set time for everything.

Time is the court of God which every creation cannot escape, no matter the faithfulness of Yahweh. We must never forget there is a time for everything.

This book defines the authority that the word carries. There's no power that can be executed without words; both words of the Creator and words of the Creatures. Psalm 138:2

A man who despises his word rejects his own power and authority.

We live what we speak and what was spoken. Proverbs 13:2, Proverbs 18:20-21.

Curses are words spoken, also blessings are words spoken. Be careful of what you speak for words are spiritual agents to execute authority and to manifest power.

This book brings the revelation of mysteries hidden in the word and the power behind it.

# CHAPTER ONE

## THE WORD OF GOD AND THE WORD OF MAN

Whatever you do or face under the sun, know that it has an end because there is nothing that is eternal on earth; even in heaven. The only one eternal is the creator Himself and His word, which He has put in command of His everything.

Time is a god, time can hear and time can also speak. Time is under the control of the Word and time has an end, for eternity is coming to creation according to the concept and vision of Elohim.

There is an end to all things outside of heaven. Let me make this clear, I did not say angels or heaven are eternal, only Elohim is eternal. It's the presence of God that makes all the beings in heaven to be eternal, and all the beings in heaven have the privilege to live endlessly than other beings who have been corrupted, for death is manufactured by sin. The result of sin is death. If you sin you will die, and you only die when you sin.

*For the wages of sin is death, but the free gift of God is eternal life in Christ Jesus Lord. Romans 6:23*

Yahweh, through His word gave man 120 years to live but the reason why God gave men 120 years to live is because He did not want man to stay long in the state of corruption and pollution because it's not His vision. How can you create something and someone comes and destroy it? This is what happened to man.

What God could have done was to grant man 120 years on earth and give him a choice if he would prefer to live eternally like in the original concept, by making a choice to accept Jesus as Lord and Saviour.

*And the Lord said, my spirit shall not always be striving with man, for he also is flesh: yet his days shall be a hundred and twenty years. Genesis 6:3*

I knew you would have asked me, how come, well! it's in making a good choice that man can live long and get back into the original concept of God by accepting Jesus Christ as the son of God who came to save us and the only way to God the Father.

One-day, master Jesus said He is older than Abraham but people did not understand and try to argued with Him.

*Jesus said unto them, very, very, I say unto you before Abraham was, I am. John 8:58*

Jesus understood the sufferings of mankind so He sent us a Helper who can bear our earthly sufferings; this is the Holy Spirit.

## THE ENERGY

Energy is the ability to make things work and there's nothing that can function without energy. I hear people say that 'this world is under the control of the enemy' this is not true. The world is under the control of the Holy Spirit no matter how much the enemy tries to frustrate the creation of God including himself as a creature who rebelled. So man is not a problem but Lucifer who is now satan . we must know that; The Holy Spirit is the master who controls everything. It's a matter of time according to the word. The Holy Spirit gave man the words we know as the bible by using human being as tools.

During Jesus Christ's time on earth, everything was under His control but when He ascended, He said; I will send you a comforter.

*I will ask the Father, and He will give you an advocate to help you and to be with you forever.*     *John 14:16*


Elohim has the ability to end all the bad you see, but time and the faithfulness of His word matter. He is full of justice and righteousness.

The bible says the Holy Spirit will be with us forever. If it says forever, then even in the tomb without a body, only with bones and spirit, He will be with us.

The resurrection Spirit raised Jesus Christ from the grave after 3 days; that is the energy giver. He is with us today and He is in charge. Can you please acknowledge Him? And say, dear Holy Spirit I love you, thank you for being there for me.

That Spirit who made the bones of Elisha give life to a dead body.

*Once some Israelites were burying a man is body. Suddenly they saw a band of raiders; so they threw the man's body into Elisha's tomb. When it touched Elisha's bones, the man came back to life and stood up on his feet. 2 King 13:21*

The same spirit gave life to Christ's body.

*He is not here; he has risen: remember how he spake unto you when he was yet in Galilee.          Luke 24:6*

The Holy Spirit is the energy that I'm talking about who makes everything to function. There is an energy that makes everything function, which we must discover to live well and enjoy the time given to us on earth by Elohim. Life is a gift of God. Ignorance of this fact is the most dangerous weapon that the enemy is using against you and I.

Many humans have not yet attained to these 120 years because of the misuse of time and the misunderstanding of the word. Listen, things do not fall apart for nothing, something has gone wrong somewhere which we must access. In the physical realm, nothing happens without word.

We live what happened spiritually, for your thought is the word. What you feed your mind with is what comes out of your mouth.

The word of God works hand in hand with time and the Spirit.

The prophet, Habakkuk understood this when he said:

*1 I will stand upon my watch, and set me upon the tower, and I will watch to see what He will say unto me. And what I shall answer when I am reproved.*

*2 and the Lord answered me, and said, write the vision, and make it plain upon tables, that he may run that read it.*

*3 For the vision is yet for an appointed time, but at the end it shall speak, and not lie: though it tarry, wait for it; because it will surely come it will not tarry.        Habakkuk 2:1-3*

The wisest king on earth once observed time and said;

There is a time for everything under the heavens

To everything there is a season and time to every purpose under the heaven:

A time to be born, and a time to die; a time to plant, and a time to pluck up that which is planted;

A time to kill, and a time heal; a time to break down, and a time to lough; a time to mourn, and a time to dance;

A time to weep and a time to lough; a time to cast away stones and a time to gather stones together; a time to embrace, and a time to refrain from embracing;

*A time to get, and a time to lose; a time to keep, and a time to cast away;*

*A time to rend, and a time to sew; a time to keep silence, and a time to speak;*

*A time to love, and a time to hate; a time of war and a time of peace. (Ecclesiastes 3:1-8).*

The earth is not eternal; neither are the creatures in it. God will surely fulfil what He said.

He does everything according to His word. If God is not acting on a matter, it's because He honours His word to act on them on the appointed time as it is written in

*'The lord replied: "write down the revelation and make it plain on tablets so that a herald may run with it. for the revelation awaits for an appointed time; it speaks of the end time and it will not prove false. Though it lingers,*

*wait for it; it will certainly come and will not delay'.* Habakkuk. 2 vs 2-3 NIV

His word will surely come to pass regardless of the circumstances. It's men who rush things not Elohim.

Whatever God told you will surely come to pass; believe it. Believing in God is like putting Him in credit, for He's faithful to His word.

What He speaks is already happening in the spirit realm but waiting to manifest in a physical realm.

Sometimes, faith is the answer to perform wonders; faith is the key to the miraculous, because when you act on God's word by faith, miracles happen. The word of God is salvation to any creature on earth; even in heaven. Yahweh exalts His word above everything; He tells people the impact of His word on them and the entire creation.

*For the word of God is alive and active, sharper than any double-edged sword, it penetrates even to dividing soul and spirit, joints, and marrow; it judges the thoughts and the attitudes of the heart. Hebrews 4:12*

In the Jeremiah, Elohim said to His Prophet.

*You have seen correctly, said the Lord, I am watching over my word to accomplish it and said the Lord to me. Jeremiah 1:12*

The fact that the world exist till today is because of the faithfulness of God to His word. There was a day, Hezekiah King of Israel made an error by disclosing the secret of the palace. God was not pleased, and because of this, He disciplined Israel for 70 years in Babylon where Daniel and his brothers found themselves.

Israel found herself in Babylon because Yahweh spoke trough a prophet and it came to pass as it was said because of a mistake made by their king. The mistakes and errors of spiritual and biological parents have cost a lot of innocents today. That is why leaders must be careful of what they do, you may pass but the next generation will face the consequences. Previous generations did not know much truth like this generation has discovered. Please, when you find the truth about your origin, do something to fix it in the name of Jesus Christ who is the solution of mankind.

Why did Elohim not kill lucifer and the other rebellious angels at the time of their disobedience? I hear many people saying why did Yahweh not kill satan and punish him immediately?

My answer to this question is:

God is a loving God and his mercy endures forever. He created Lucifer, he gave him time at least to survive but since he became Satan and worst of all, because of his jealousy he touched God's other creatures who were innocents. Many are suffering innocently because they have refused to bow to the enemy. lucifer became the real enemy of man when he saw the position given to man by the Creator, now he is no more lucifer but satan the deceiver and the father of all lies, the wicked one.

Actually he was well placed in the kingdom of Yahweh our father (Ezekiel 28:13-15), but he admired the throne of his creator, he said I will build my own throne on top of my creator, meaning I will be greater than my creator! No one can be greater than the creator; He lived before everything existed. He was alone first then he made a plan to create angels & humans and others living things.

Angels were created by God and Lucifer was among the creatures just like other angelic being, and he was privileged to have a position in heaven. Yahweh existed before the invisible world and the visible, the unseen world and the physical world. lucifer changed from lucifer to satan, He grew worse and worse.

Satan means deceiver, with his deceits he was able to deceive many around the world by telling them that he is a master. he says Yahweh hate his creatures and he loves them which is a very big lie. The great master, Jesus

Christ of Nazareth described satan as a thief in John 10:10.

Let us define the characteristics of the enemy according to this verse.

**Who is a Thief**

A thief is the one who take things that does not belong to him without permission. In this verse (John 10:10), there are three words used to describe Satan which are; killer, stealer, and destroyer.

A thief will prefer to leave you empty, and take everything that belongs to you by force. That is why emptiness is a proof that the enemy is at work. Observe where there's an emptiness in your live, also observe what you had before and you don't have any more, it is a proof that the enemy has done something to you.

## Declaration

**Father, in the name of Jesus, I pray everything the enemy has stolen from me and my family, or any area of my life, I take them back in the mighty name of Jesus Christ.**

## Who is a killer?

A killer is someone who hates life. What is life? Life is the fact of activities that a being can do. We have a simple example which is; when the body of a person is dead, we can observe that the body does not move, this means the body is dead. Now imagine if it says the soul that sin is will die.

The death of a soul means separation between man and God, for man can only live when he's connected to his creator, and the first mission of Satan is to separate man from his creator so that he can perish. Man is forgiven but not Satan. Satan is judged and condemned and he is waiting for the time.

By God's privilege, I am a deliverance minister. From my experience, I hear demons say 'stop tormenting me for my time has not yet come'. Death of the flesh is separation of the spirit of man and his body, but death of the spirit is separation between man and His creator. The reason people die without attaining to the 120 years is because of ignorance of some facts of the purpose of creation.

It is the mission of the enemy to separate every spirit from their creator, to misled them to worship him. This was what he wanted from the beginning and for this he was casted out of heaven. Life is only where Elohim is, far away there is no life.

For you to have life, you must stand in God's presence. The body you have has a set time before it expires. The purpose of diseases and sicknesses is to limit the days of the human body, by making it suffer. For every evil spirit is trained for these three missions; to kill, steal, and destroy.

In my next book; True Freedom, I will share more details about this.

**Prayer Declaration**

**In the name of Jesus, I decree life into every area of my life that is experiencing lifelessness, in the name of Jesus Amen.**

## Who is a destroyer?

A destroyer is somebody who hates goodness or order; he messes up every good and orderly thing he sees. The enemy have destroyed many destinies because of ignorance, our fathers and elders did not know the truth as we do today. Many are victims of their ignorance; many are facing the consequences of the errors of our forefathers.

I pray for this generation to be restored to their creator, for the next generation depend on this generation for things to gain shape.

We cannot point only to the mistakes of our elders; we must also point to their good deeds, which we must imitate for the sustainability of this generation and the next to come.

## Prayer Declaration

**I speak restoration to any destroyed thing in my life, in my family, and in my business and career, in the name of Jesus Christ. Amen!**

## Satan is an Opposer

He opposes anything good that comes to man. Yahweh wants man to live a peaceful and joyful life, but the enemy opposes this by using different strategies against man so he cannot live in peace and joy.

It's very important to have the knowledge of Yahweh to enable us oppose and resist the enemy, because even our Lord Jesus Christ when He was on earth, He resisted satan through the knowledge of His father Yahweh. By this we understand that to win any battle against the enemy we should have the word of God which the enemy fears the most.

By God's word, we can defeat our enemy, because the only weapon for victory is the word of God.

Yahweh is showing the people of the earth how to have His word so that they can live. Eternal life is the word of Yahweh, nothing else.

*My people are destroyed for the lack of knowledge; because thou hast rejected knowledge, I will also reject thee, that thou shalt be no priest to me; seeing thou hast forgotten the law of thy God, I will also forget thy children. Hosea 4:6 KJV.*

When we reject God's word, we become completely dead. If our grandfather Adam had obeyed the instructions given to him by Yahweh, death would have not entered amongst humanity.

Lack of Obedience to God's word is what brought chaos on earth and in many things including your life. The word of God is the light of the entire creation, the word of God is a light to your life, and anything we do without the presence of the word of God cannot prosper. Why do I say so? Because there is no one who can walk in darkness with the absences of light. A life lead by God's word is a successful life; there is no one from Genesis to Revelation who was great without being a doer of the word of God. All great people in the bible who did wonders and made great history, did so with and in obedience to the word of God, Everyone from Abraham to John.

Without God's word the universe is in darkness. The enemy knows this truth therefore he's doing everything in his means to twist the Bible. Be careful of what you read or learn because, it's not every word you read or hear that is for your benefit. You become what you consume because what you read and hear possesses your spirit, and what is contained in your spirit becomes your imagination, and what becomes your imagination becomes your thoughts, and your thought is what defines your life and personality. You are who you think you are.

Some preachers, who are serving the enemy have created a demonic theology to confuse humanity; mostly those who do not have the light in them. I mean people who have not yet accepted the

Lord Jesus Christ as their personal saviour to their very hearts. It is He, the word of God that became flesh to save mankind.

I know you are going to ask yourself how come Jesus Christ is the word and the enemy can still twist God's word? He Himself said it, that many will come in my name.

*For many will come in my name, claiming, I am the Messiah; and will deceive many. Matthew 24:5 KJV.*

After our Lord Jesus prayed for 40 days and 40 nights, the enemy came to tempt Him, our model. If we don't follow our Lord Jesus' model what model should we follow?

He is the only one who can save us, we better follow Him as our model. The experiences of those who followed Him faithfully gives us an example of the journey we are into.

The real opposer is satan who uses people who are weak and are blinded to the truth. I'm saying the enemy also uses people who don't have the light of God, why? Because he can easily penetrate where there is darkness.

A place of light is a difficult place for the enemy to operate. Can a Christian be use by the devil? Yes, if he or she is distracted, the enemy can use that person as a tool to destroy someone's life or his or her own.

That is why it's so important to pay attention to actions made by people who surround us.

Whether they are used by satan or it's their human character, the enemy can attack you through a person who is closer to you such as a family member, friend, classmate, colleague, workmate, your children, even parents, if they are not godly.

parents can be used of the devil to lay a curse on your life or to make your life miserable.

In the following chapter, I described the impact of our parent's word in our life.

## Satan is an Accuser

He accuses everyone who is not a doer of God's word.

One day, he went to ask permission from God to touch Job, the faithful servant of God.

Why did he ask? Because if you are a doer of the word of God the enemy has no right to touch you unless if, he is given permission, as he went to ask God to touch Job.

⁶ One day the angels[a] came to present themselves before the Lord, and Satan[b] also came with them. ⁷ The Lord said to Satan, "Where have you come from?"

Satan answered the Lord, "From roaming throughout the earth, going back and forth on it."

⁸ Then the Lord said to Satan, "Have you considered my servant Job? There is no one on earth like him; he is blameless and upright, a man who fears God and shuns evil."

⁹ "Does Job fear God for nothing?" Satan replied. ¹⁰ "Have you not put a hedge around him and his household and everything he has? You have blessed the work of his hands, so that his flocks and herds are spread

*throughout the land. ¹¹ But now stretch out your hand and strike everything he has, and he will surely curse you to your face."*

*¹² The L{ORD} said to Satan, "Very well, then, everything he has is in your power, but on the man, himself do not lay a finger."*     Job 1:6-12   NIV

He uses malice to cause many to sin, so he can accuse them of not been doers of the word of their creator.

Again, he went to Jesus Christ the son of God, using the same words he was preaching but twisting the meaning and using the word of God in a corrupt way.

We must not forget that the devil knows the bible well. This should not be a surprise because he knew and knows the mysteries that are hidden in the word.

I strongly advise us all to be doers of the word of God so that we can prevent the enemy from gaining access to us. He went to Job to seek how he can destroy him but he could not, why? Because brother Job was a doer of God's word.

There are many prayer warriors in our generation but only few are doers of God's word. Sometimes, we don't receive answers to our prayers on time because we didn't use it the right way. The impactful prayer is the prayer that is focused on God's written word.

If you want to see the effectiveness of your prayers, pray according to God's word, you will see much results. The bible say we should pray with understanding.

*"What is it then? I will pray with the spirit, and I will pray with the*

*understanding also: I will sing with the spirit, and I will sing with the understanding also." 1 Corinthians 14:15 (KJV)*

Beloved, the truth is we can't have understanding without God's word. The creation, the universe, and all the activities happening in it, all are mysteries, and mysteries can only be revealed by the word of God.

**Praying by the Holy Spirit.**

The Holy Spirit helps us to pray in accordance to the word of God. Though He's our helper, the word is the road of command, meaning the word precedes everything. The Holy Spirit brings the word to manifestation, so it's impossible for Him to work or walk with a person who is not a doer of the word. Whoever is disobedient to God's word does not live in the truth and the person who does not live in the truth cannot please God. Disobedience to God's word always grieves the Holy Spirit because, He is the Spirit of truth and it is by truth a man can be set free.

The Spirit of God is there to set us free from the lies of the enemy through Jehovah's word. When the world was sick, the only thing it needed was the truth and what is this truth? The truth is a person, what kind of person? The person of Jesus Christ; the word that became flesh.

*The word became flesh and made his dwelling among us. We have seen his glory the one and only son, who came from the father, full of grace and truth. John 1:14-18*

The word of the creator is full of Grace and Truth. This are the two things the earth needs. Before you find truth, you must find Grace.

For Elohim to save man, firstly, He gave him Grace then the Truth came to make man understand the difference between lies and truth. The earth was full of lies from the enemy and it needed the truth to receive salvation.

What is Truth? And what is Grace?

Truth is to set free and grace is to be qualified.

For Elohim so loved the world, He gave grace to every of His creation. The truth has to be believed, but Grace has been freely given to everyone.

Let us look at Grace before I define truth.

# WHAT IS GRACE?

## Biblical Definition

Grace is a spontaneous gift from Elohim to His people. It is an undeserved and unexpected favour.

## My Definition of Grace

It is the expression of the unconditional love of the creator to His creation.

Yahweh could have burnt the earth and every creature in it, but He expressed His love through Grace.

## Dictionary Definition

Grace is a way of getting or doing something effortlessly. To become a child of God or become born again is effortless, It's a simple action; all you have to do is confess.

**Only say this: Lord Jesus Christ I receive you as my personal LORD AND SAVIOUR from today. Forgive my sins, thank you for dying on the cross for me. Amen!!!**

This confession does not take even a minute, but it can change the entire life of a man.

Salvation came to man but victory came to angels. Are angels' sinners? The answer is no. Angels are very compassionate to man and this is the kind of compassion Jehovah has towards man. Since angels are here on earth; they understand and see the suffering of mankind. Because of this, they rejoiced to see man receive salvation. Men needed salvation because they were sinners.

Please if you've never receive Jesus Christ as your Lord and Saviour, say this prayer with me:

**Lord Jesus Christ I receive you as my personal Lord and saviour. From today, forgive my sins. I thank you for dying on the cross for me, enter into my heart**

**and remove the evil in me and make me your child. Amen!!!**

The root of the word grace is 'Chen' in Hebrew which is from the root word 'Chanan' which means to stand in kindness. It means God showed His kindness to Humanity.

Grace is for everyone, believer or unbelievers. Grace came for everyone; it's not peculiar to a group of people. Grace is the gate and the door to the truth. When you recognize Grace, it will lead you to the truth. That you are saved doesn't mean you know the truth, that is the reason why our Lord Jesus said the Holy Spirit will teach us all things.

Grace is a privilege to everyone but truth must be taught. but *the Comforter, which is the Holy Ghost, whom the Father will send in my name, He shall teach you all things, and bring all things to your remembrance, whatsoever I have said unto to you. John 14:26 KJV.*

## TRUTH

### Dictionary Definition

**It is the quality of being or a state of a person**

### My Definition

Truth is inside of Elohim, He sent truth in the form of a man to save His creation.

Jesus Christ is inside of Elohim that He has released to save His creatures from the lies and deceit of the enemy, and there's no way the word of God will not have an impact.

The word of Elohim created everything. It is the word of God that knows the details about creation. Therefore, if we want to know about any and everything, we should seek to know the truth which is Jesus Christ who is called the son of God.

If we claim to know God the father and we do not know the son, then we don't know Him, for a tree is known by its fruit. What you produce describes your kind. So if we are to describe Elohim, we must describe Him by Jesus for He is inside of Elohim.

We cannot separate the word of a person from the person, it's impossible because your word and you are one. Your word is the same as you, what you speak describes the kind of person you are. Therefore, we cannot separate Yahweh and Jesus.

**Jesus, Philip said to master Jesus "Show us the father" and that will be enough for us and Master Jesus answered Him, even after I have been among you such a long time? Anyone who has seen me has seen the father? How can you say show us the father? John 14:8-9 (NIV)**

Here, Jesus said He is the father Himself; then how can we say Jesus Christ is not God the Father? What does the word of God look like?

**For the word God is quick, and powerful, and sharper than any two-edged sword, piercing even to the dividing asunder of the soul and spirit,**

**and of the joints and marrow, and is a discerner of the thoughts and intents of the heart. Hebrews 4 vs 12 (KJV)**

The word of God will judge the world. God will judge each creature through His word. So if the word became a person called Jesus, then He's the one who will judge mankind.

**Nothing in all creation is hidden from God's sight. Everything is uncovered and laid bare before the eyes of him to whom we must give account. Hebrews 4:13 (NIV)**

It is Jesus who will judge and condemn the enemy, for the enemy will be judged and sentenced to 1000 years in the prison as stated by the word of God.

**When the thousand years are over, the enemy will be released from his prison.    Rev 20:7-10**

We must surrender our human ability to the word of God so that we may find the light. If we have the word of God in us, everything will be simple. Praying is good but an effective prayer is a prayer that's based on God is word.

The truth is revealed trough the word, the Holy Spirit manifest the word. the truth is light and clarification that is why the Lord said He will teach you His word because The truth is Jesus Himself.

T HERE ARE WORDS OF MAN AND THE WORD OF GOD.

As I previously said, word is an instrument of power. Words are spiritual agents according to Jesus Christ; since He is the creator, let's follow His definition.

Words have the power to project. You can be far, but your word can have more impact than even your presence.

Mind your words.

Listen to how Jesus described the word from his mouth:

*It is the spirit that quickened; the flesh profited nothing: the words that I speak unto you, they are spirit, and they are life. John 6:63 (KJV)*

The state of your fleshly life depends on the word you speak. If you speak the opposite of life which is death, surely you will see death surrounding you, for death has agents. Sickness is the agent of death because the mission of sickness is to frustrate your mortal body until it disappears from the earth.

Your words have power to affect your spirit, body and soul.

# Where does Words Come from?

Words are from the unseen world. There was a man who was blind, when Jesus opened his eyes, what he saw first were men like trees. I like this passage because it shows the real state of man. We are like trees and our life depends on the kind of water we receive to survive. If polluted water is poured on us, we become polluted; this is the same in the spirit. How can you have produced fruits, if you are not a tree? Our Lord Jesus is happy when we bear fruits.

*Herein my Father glorified, that ye bear much fruits; so shall ye be my disciples. John 15:8 KJV*

According to some spiritual definitions, the word of God is interpreted as water.

There was a day Jesus said you are sanctified by the word I'm preaching to you.

In the spirit realm, we grow every time whether in a wrong or in a right direction. The results are the fruits we bear, which is as a result of where the source of our water is connected in the spiritual realm.

Polluted and clean water are both words, and this is the energy I'm speaking about, we are influenced by what we survive on in the spiritual realm.

The results are like fruits; the fruits we provide surely define the tree we're connected to. Both words carry authority, I mean words of men and the word of God. Things are spoken from your mind before you act physically, and that can be also the voice of the enemy, it's important to be taught the word of God so that you know if you are receiving pollution water or clean water." water means the word"

We are taught by the Holy Spirit by a genuine man of God but the great teacher is the Holy Spirit even the man of God has been and he is taught by the Holy Spirit.

Now let's study the word of man.

Please, keep reading, a secret is about to be revealed to you and your life is about to turn around for good, you shall not be the same again after reading this book.

The one who gave the inspiration of this material has a specific mission for you, this book was written for you.

# Word of man

The word to mankind is a means of communication.

The ability to speak is the instrument God gave man to communicate to themselves. Word is the instrumental authority given to man by which he can exercise authority over creation and communicate to His kind.

God gave man the responsibility to look after the Garden of Eden and everything in it. The universe exists under the authority of man not under the authority of God because it is given to him, for He commanded man to have dominion over all things that He created. Don't get me wrong, I did not say God do not have authority over the universe; what I'm telling you is God gave you the universe to rule over it.

Each individual rules over his life, the biggest problem we have as men is the ignorance of the truth which is in the word. The secret of everything is in the mystery of the word we speak and what God speaks.

*26 Then God said, "Let Us make man in Our image, according to Our likeness; let them have dominion over the fish of the sea, over the birds of the air, and over the cattle, over [a]all the earth and over every creeping thing that creeps on the earth."* ²⁷ *So God created man in His own image; in the image of God He created him; male and female He created them.* ²⁸ *Then God blessed them, and God said to them, "Be fruitful and multiply; fill the earth and subdue it; have dominion over the fish of the sea, over the birds of the air, and over every living thing that* [b]*moves on the earth." Genesis 1:26-28 KJV*

This world and everything in it belongs to man. They were given to us. This is where it all started: Yahweh created the angels and the heavens, among the angels lucifer rebelled against God and some angels went with him.

God could have created the earth and another heaven and destroy the previous ones, but to show his power and showcase His glory and to prove to all creation that He is God, He created the heavens and the earth in seven days.

I strongly believe this is what distinguishes Him as a Creator, for it was better to make something bigger than what already existed, so that they can acknowledge that He's almighty. Therefore, He created the universe to prove that.

This is just my concept and observation, for we cannot put God in the box, by saying this what and how he does, He's capable of making something greater than what we see and know.

The power of dominion and rulership is under the tongue of man only if he exercises his authority. By doing so, lucifer who is the father of lies got jealous and plotted his downfall and became the greatest enemy of man.

Lucifer cannot be an enemy of God, because it does not take a second for God to destroy and erase him from existence. He is the enemy of man and other angels in heaven by fighting man and angels. This is where he automatically became an enemy of God, because he fights his creatures.

God cannot fight satan because it will be like Him reducing Himself, but He strengthens those who have come out of ignorance to fight him. The last time satan was defeated forever was on the cross of Calvary through Jesus Christ, the first born of the new world called the world of believers, making it possible for man to accept Jesus as his Lord and Saviour.

The enemy is defeated true the blood of the lamb alleluia!

Man is the centre of all things and there is somebody who hates him. The evil we face is caused by the devil who's jealous of man's authority. You are given authority over all of God's creation.

No one is less than the other, the fact is we are given different purposes to fulfil on earth. Whoever undermines another creature does not yet understand the rules of creation. Apart from this, the one who turned against our creator should be despised always.

There is authority in you, you were created with it, you were born with that power in you. You're from power, created in power, and for power, also to show power.

We lost it during the fall, but it's totally restored by the work of Jesus Christ. Now, we are back to the origin, by accepting Jesus Christ.

It was through the word of Adam that animals received their names and identity. If man gave animals their names; it means it is man who identify all creatures.

So identify your life and your generation by your words, speak greatness and speak victory, don't speak defeat for you will be defeated.

The size of your life is defined by understanding the secrets available to you through this book.

Speak life, and you will live, speak death; you will surely die, your life is designed by your word.

Every area of your life depends on the knowledge of this secret.

Speak today and you will reap tomorrow.

Your words are seeds that you are going to eat in the future.

Create a great future with the words you speak today. The future, maybe today later or tomorrow.

Without man, nothing on earth would have been identified. There's a principle on earth that whatsoever lacks a name on earth is unidentifiable, and anything without identity is suspicious. It's identity that describes a creature, that is why the emphasis of Jesus's teachings is for you to gain your original identity.

*And Adam gave names to all cattle, and to the fowl of the air, and to every beast of the field; but for Adam there was not found a help meet for him.     Genesis 2 vs 20 (KJV)*

There is no way Adam could have named all these creatures without practicing the word. If you undermine your own words, it means you undermine your own authority. A man who do not respect his words, despises his own authority.

God has given us authority through our words by using our tongue, we exercise authority.

We have the power to give life and to take away life.

**Proverbs 18:21 KJV.**

The tongue is the smallest member of the body but it is the greatest member in the realm of the spirit.

Wrong thoughts and motives behind words are the cause of bad results on earth. The greatest instrument of miracles for man is his own words. A prudent man is the person who values and controls his words.

Words are spiritual agents that determines our tomorrow. Your word can travel to your future before you arrive in it. What you confess concerning your business, marriage, career, family, etc. will become a reality in the physical realm.

So, endeavour to speak good and positive words always and over situations.

We were made for positivity not negativity. Regardless of what is happening, you can create a world of your own with your words. Your words are prophecies of your life.

**<u>Prayer confession</u>**
- Lord Jesus, I thank you for this revelation.
- I confess good words and I renounced every bad word I've said in the past.
- I speak good words and growth in every area of my life.
- I renounce every sickness and disease that I have confessed and

attracted by my own words in the mighty name of Jesus Christ Amen.

# The Word of God

Whoever is not a doer of God's word, displeases God, and whoever does the word of God pleases God.

What is the word of God? The word of God is an instrument of power. No creature in heaven or on earth can act outside of the word of God.

Whoever act outside of the word of Yahweh violate the rules of God and there are consequences for violating God's word. God has placed this fact at the centre of everything, With His Word He created time.

# CHAPTER TWO

## WORD AND TIME

Word and time are the greatest judges of God. Jehovah uses these means to rule His creations, for He created everything through them.

God created time when He made the heavens and the earth. Where did Yahweh live before He created the heavens and the earth?

He lived in eternity, and in eternity there is no time, eternity is the country of God alone.

As believers in Jesus Christ, we are guaranteed eternal life after this passing age, and the new Jerusalem is where we will all live one day.

I wish for that time to come now alleluia! We will be singing a new song in front of the majestic throne of our Father. Come Lord Jesus Christ, you who overcame the world, indeed we are desperate for you.

There's a proof of when He created time, but there's no proof of when God created the word. This means the word was with Him in eternity, please read the book of Genesis carefully.

God created time for justice since, He gave men freedom of choice. humans and angels can decide to serve God or not to serve Him. Yahweh will not enslave His creatures; He loves all unconditionally.

This is the reason why some angels followed lucifer when he was casted out of heaven. God also gave free will to humans. This is why Jesus Christ will continue standing at the door of your heart until you open the door for Him. He does not force Himself into anyone's life; He comes in with your permission.

Listen to what He said

***Behold, I stand at the door, and knock: if any man hears my voice, and open the door, I will come into to him, and will sup with him, and he with me. Revelation 3:20 KJV***

Jesus Christ who is God the son, came to earth in the form of man, He didn't force anyone to receive salvation, if you chose to be saved you are saved, if you refuse salvation through Jesus Christ, then you are lost and punishment awaits you in the lake of fire.

# Time

Time was not in order for the universe to function, there was only eternity, and God had to create a chronological means of living for human. Since man was created differently from heavenly beings;

Time talks and time can be silent. The reason why we always remember our past mistake when we are about to make the same mistakes again, time talks to us.

The problem is, you never understand and pay attention to time, Time talks to you. Time is a creature just like you and I

You can communicate with time, since it is a fellow creature. Remember you cannot manipulate time. but you can manage time.

When I say manage, I mean to cooperate with time.

A good manager is proven by his abilities of cooperation with the people he or she leads.

Your entire life is under your management, you are privileged to live 120 years on earth, and we cannot speak about years if there is no time. It means there should be a corporation. Live for something, don't live for nothing, positively maximise each minute, seconds, month, week, year that you are given.

You can also control time through the word of God, our maker.

The word of God has the capacity to controls time.

If you speak the word of God, time has no option than to obey you.

## Prayer confession

Time and seasons hear me as your fellow creature, in the years, weeks, months and days to come, from now on, bring good things for my benefits in Jesus Name. Amen!!!

# CHAPTER THREE

## ETERNAL LIFE IS HIDDEN IN THE WORD OF GOD

The word of God is eternal life. Jesus spoke to one of his disciples, 'man shall not live by bread alone', meaning there's a food of the Spirit that gives life and there's a food that nourishes the body, but life is in the Spirit.

*But he answered and said, it's written, man shall not live by bread alone, but by every word that proceeded out of the mouth of God.*

*Matthew 4:4 KJV*

The word of God is the Spirit, our master made it clear in Hebrews 4:12. When we use the word of God, they travel unseeingly, since they are spirit. They act invisibly to manifest it's intended purpose.

It is important that every time we pray against the enemy, we should do so using the word of God.

# CHAPTER FOUR

## THE AUTHORITY OF A MAN

Man, also has his own words, this is the ability given by the creator to communicate with things and people around us. Adam was given the power to name every animal in the garden of Eden, through the power of the word. God gave man power to be fruitful, to multiply, replenish, subdue, and dominate. Genesis 1:28

There's no authority without words, for authority is executed by words through the tongue. Have you realized that when you speak with your mouth, there is a movement of the tongue that releases breath? Put your hand to your mouth, you will feel breathe coming out. When God formed man, he was unconscious till He breathed into his nostril, then he became a living being. This means that life came after breathing in him, and the breath symbolizes the Holy Spirit.

Jesus said the words he was preaching they were spirit and they are life.

*It is the spirit that quicken; the flesh profit nothing: the words that I speak to you, they are spirit and life. John 6:63KJV*

When speaking, there's a release of power from the realm of the supernatural hence, we must be careful of any word we speak.

Since, it's through the word that the breath of life comes, then there is a secret we must discover here.

Whatever you speak is accompanied by the breath of life, which gives authority to whatever you are addressing.

You are responsible for every word you speak because it is from your mouth and when the word is spoken you can't take it back.

words execute and it will do has intended.

**Prayer confession**

**Heavenly Father, every contradicting word I have spoken against my life**

and destiny, I reverse them in Jesus Name.

Amen!!!

# CHAPTER FIVE
## HOW TO BENEFIT FROM THE WORD OF GOD

1. Practice and stand bold in the word of God. Let the word of God be your life style, if you want to live an extraordinary life, be a doer of God's word. Before reading the bible, pray that the Holy Spirit assists you in reading, for better understanding. It simple, just ask Him, just say please Holy Spirit help me. He will immediately act on your request because it pleases Him to teach you God's word.

2. Use the word in every circumstances of life. When you use the word, you will always overcome. Living in the word of God means living a life of victory. The word is a better place to hide because there, satan can never see you. The word of God is light, once you live in the word, darkness can never come to you.

It has always been an intention of God for you to benefit from His word.

If you not benefiting from His word, you are not a doer of His word.

If you are a doer, then claim your right in every domain.

# CHAPTER SIX

## HOW TO IMPACT WITH YOUR WORDS

To make impact with your word, you must value your word. I said in my introduction that a man who does not value his word despises his own authority because there's no authority that can be execute without the word.

For your word to make impact on earth and in your life, you must carry God's word in your mouth. You must let the word of Yahweh reside in you always.

When the word of God becomes available in your mouth, your tongue becomes a dangerous weapon against the kingdom of darkness. You will be revealing inspirational mysteries that is unheard of in the world. You will generate power as never seen on the earth.

The bible says in proverbs 13:2 (KJV) 'you shall eat the fruits of your mouth'. It's only when you associate with

Elohim's word that you will begin to experience the supernatural.

Early in my ministry, I realized that when preaching, people will start speaking in tongues and will begin to pray before I finished preaching, I use to wonder what was happening. Now, I understand that the words I preach are not mine. The owner of the words manifested and revealed the energy behind His word.

Be a discipled person, a mouth that speaks too much, always makes mistakes.

Learn when to speak and when not to speak.

# CHAPTER SEVEN
## THE POWER OF YOUR TONGUE

The tongue is a member of the body which has authority to give life or death to our future. The future depends on what we speak concerning ourselves by using our tongue.

Many are victims of their own words because that they have used it ignorantly without knowing they were cursing their own selves.

Every time we speak words, there is an air that is released through the mouth, and these words are agents of the spiritual realm. Words have power in the invisible world. Jesus Christ describes it to His disciples this way:

*The spirit gives life; the flesh counts for nothing. The words I have spoken to you –they are full of Spirit and life. John 6:63 NIV*

Words put a man in connection with the spiritual world, and since words are spiritual agents according to how Jesus describes it in John 6;63

*It is the spirit that quicken; the flesh profited nothing: the words that I speak unto you, they are spirit, and they are life. (KJV).*

Look at the words of Jesus, He revealed himself to His followers, So we could learn from Him for better understanding. We must not take our words for granted because they are also spirits.

When we check how Jesus describes the word 'spirit', He is referring to the human spirit, the spirit of man; because the spirit of man carries small letter while the Holy Spirit carries capital letter. I used KJV because it's the original translation.

Jesus Christ was referring to Himself as a human being that took the form of man to live among mortal men. It's true that He's God, but during His time on earth, He was a mortal man. That's why He died, if He was not mortal, He wouldn't have died.

Some people say He was fully God, that's why He could endure the pain of the cross and conquer sin, others say Jesus was half man and half God, that's why He succeeded in conquering sin; this is not true.

If it were true, let me ask you a question; who is the father of Adam? Didn't we originate from Adam? If yes them, we are also half spirit and half man because no one knows who gave birth to Adam.

Can you please tell me who fathered Adam? From the beginning, when Yahweh created Adam, Eve was not there but taken from the Rib of Adam. If

Adam does not have a father, and then we are from the spiritual world through Adam.

Jesus's greatest mission on earth was for man to regain his original position. He came to save mankind. When we speak your words and not the word of God, it's in small letter (spirit) because what you speak is a spirit.

Your words are spiritual agents; you send them on a mission. When you send them, they execute the mission either negative or positive. That's why you must be careful of what you speak.

I hear some people say 'I cannot make it'. My brother and sister, because you say cannot make it, you will never make it until you speak positive words that you will make it.

I also hear some ladies say 'marriage is not mine', since you've said it's not yours, it will never be yours. When you begin to face rejections and deceptions don't accuse anybody. You create your world with your own words. They were given to you as the power of creation, speak good things about yourself and you will see them manifest in the future if you believe in the authority behind your words.

Whatever you don't possess by word you can never possess it by the spirit. The battles that you don't win by your own word you can never win them spiritually.

**Proverbs 13:2 KJV**

**from the fruits of their lips people enjoy good things, but the unfaithful have an appetite for violence.**

You shall eat the fruits of your mouth, if you speak good things, you'll eat good things, if you speak bad things, you'll eat bad things.

# CHAPTER EIGHT

## WORDS FROM OUR PARENTS

We have both spiritual parents and biological parents. Both of these parents have an impact on the life of a person.

### Biological parents

Parent are gods to their children.

Mind what you speak to them.

It's not good to complain about your child or your children, because every words you speak concerning your child it will affect him or her. Why can't you just pray to God who assigned you to be a parent to that child? He has the solution to any matter you are facing in your family.

Bless your children, love them, don't under estimate your children but encourage them.

Many children are victims of what have been spoken by their parents. Words like - you are a shame to our family. If you as a father or mother have spoken against any of your children, please reverse your words and begin to speak good things concerning your children.

Again, never use any negative words against your children, for they will face the consequences of what you speak over them. The bible says that parents are the gods of their children. You have the power to bless them or curse them therefore, be careful of what you speak over them.

## Spiritual Parents

Today we are having many issues about this topic: the bible didn't mention only biological parents but also spiritual parents, that means we have to pay attention to this matter as well.

Who is a spiritual parent?

My answer to this question is as followed: a spiritual parent is a person who introduce you to the spiritual world.

whatever religion you are, since I'm a Christian so I will speak about it in a Christian way.

A spiritual parent is the one who introduce you to Christianity,

He is a person whom the Lord has assigned to feed you His word for the benefit of your soul.

**Spiritual parent in leadership**

Anyone who introduced you into the leadership that you are leading today spiritually, that is your spiritual parent.

You can never have two spiritual parents, only one, unless your spiritual parent is dead there you can seek for one by the leading of the Spirit with much convictions and spiritual proves.

Let me clarify on this;

**Mentors and Parents**

There is a different between a mentor and a spiritual parent, you can have more than one mentor, but not spiritual parent, a parent will always be one.

A child can never have two mothers and fathers only one mother and one father.

Mentors are people you draw inspiration from in different areas of life.

God is not an author of disorder but order.

**Children**

Also, as a child, you have to obey those whom God has given you as god upon the earth, so you may live long. You need to obey your parents so that you don't cause them to make a mistake by cursing you. If you were used to disobeying your parents and they are no more alive, please ask God for forgiveness. keep reading for better understanding. You can pray on your knees after reading this chapter, if your parents are alive and you don't talk to them, please just humble yourself and go ask for forgiveness so you can live long. if they are evil, you can ask for forgiveness and stand far in distance to protect yourself from their evils.

When you disobey your parents, it is God you're disobeying and the consequence is death. God gave a command in His word to everyone who will disobeys their parents.

God didn't do a mistake to give you that mother and father no matter their status and appearance, we didn't choose parents but God choses for us, and God can only choose what is best for you.

Your parents are not an error of God, because God never create an error, and everything God creates and does are perfect.

Honour thy father and thy mother: that thy days may be long upon the land which the LORD thy God giveth thee. Exodus 20:12 KJV

You shall fear everyone his mother and his father and keep my Sabbaths I am the Lord your God.

**Leviticus 19: 3KJV**

Children obey your parents in the Lord: for this right. Honour thy father and thy mother, which is the first commandment with promise; that it may be well with you thou may live long on earth.

**Ephesians 6:1-3 KJV**

# CHAPTER NINE

## WORDS AND MOUTH

The two most dangerous members of the body are the tongue and the mouth.

Word is the instrument that Yahweh chose for man to practice the ability to express himself. That is why it requires a man's mouth to curse and to bless. All that is needed for curse and for blessing is word and mouth.

*In the beginning God created the heavens and the earth and the earth was formless and void; and darkness was upon the face of the face of the deep and the Spirit of God moved upon the face of the water and God said, let there be light: and there was light. Genesis1:1-3KJV*

There were actions that God took, one is to create. Then he sent his Spirit to move to check what to do next, and then later He spoke, meaning; He released His words.

The whole act of creation is what God said. It simply means God was speaking to create.

If you were cursed, know very well that it was by words because there's no curse without words spoken. For a curse to be a curse, it requires words, for a blessing to be a blessing, it also requires words.

Our ancestors-built altars, after building them, they spoke over it after putting something valuable. For the altar to be powerful it has to be accompanied by words.

Some families are facing the consequences of the words spoken by one of their member who joined certain branch of the dark world.

When man disobeyed God in the garden of Eden, God used words to judge Adam and his wife. To avoid confusion, God didn't curse Adam and his wife, but they suffered the consequences of their disobedience. When He created Adam, He clearly told him that if you eat the tree of knowledge of good and evil, you will surely die.

> Comment [h]: please sir, I don't understand this sentence

The reason God prevented Adam from eating from the tree of the knowledge of good and evil is because the word pronounced by God is his principle.

The human planet became a cursed place; it was also by the word that the human planet became a blessed place. When God blessed the earth again, he used His word.

Psalm 107:20-22 KJV

He sent His word to heal them and deliver them from destructions. Use your tongue carefully.

## CHAPTER TEN
### WE ARE GODS

Everything we see in this world is created by what was spoken or what we speak now. Do not be your own witch, do not be your own demon.

Before, you didn't know this secret, but now you know. Please mind your words, don't curse any one including yourself, and always use your words to bless people.

There are so many people who are victims of spoken words. In the realm of the spirit, there's no sacrifice that is made without words. There are always words spoken on the altar to make the altar stronger, every altar function by words.

Words invokes spirits and activate covenants on altars.

The knowledge you receive from a teacher at school or preacher at church are possible by words. The words you hear builds a personality in you. Have you noticed? The person you listening to most is who you'll begin to behave like.

What you hear frequently will always form a part of your personality.

The reason why the enemy is a deceiver is because he does not want us to discover the implication of the negative words we speak over our lives, over people and situations.

The strongest covenant is in the word of God, and God can never break the covenant of his word, for He is a faithful God.

Even our greatest master Jesus Christ, when He was on the cross, He said it is finished while He was dying. He had to speak mysteries hidden in the word that we have to discover.

**What is the impact of words?**

What the mouth speaks make an agreement with the spiritual world to bring it to fulfilment. Words are a means to manifest power and exercise authority. There is no authority that is exercised without words being spoken.

I believe that this authority works when you recognize it. The King of kings said that He saw the enemy falling like lighting but I have given you authority and power to trample upon serpent and scorpions and over all the power of the enemy and nothing shall by any means harm you.

Whosoever has accepted Jesus Christ as his or her personal Lord and Saviour has received this power.

**How to Exercise this Authority?**

To exercise this authority given by Jesus, you must use His word because His word is an unfailing weapon that a man must have in his armoury.

Yahweh spoke to prophet Isaiah that His word cannot return to Him without it being accomplished.

**So is my word that goes out of my mouth: it will not return to me empty.**

**Jeremiah 55:11 KJV**

It was through His word that the universe was created. If the creator Himself uses His word, then we His creation should not be ignorant of this fact.

A life without word is a life without destiny, and any destiny bad or good is determine by spoken words. Most of the challenges our generation is facing today are things spoken and done by past generations.

That is why it's very important to search your past generation, for you to have a right standing. Meaning check your foundation or your origin. It is unnecessary to go ahead while the foundation is still faulty. Have you noticed that there are some people who no matter how far they go, they always return to the same position. This is a foundational problem.

I will recommend to you my next book; **My Vision my Home by Prophet Hiddekel Jephte.**

The enemy may have a legal standing in your life, family, career, business, marriage, relationship or ministry because of what was said or done in the past by someone in your linage.

Your ancestors may have given the enemy a legal permission to do whatever they want. Many of the previous generations were ignorant; they did things without thinking of how it will impact the next generation.

Whatever you do, your next generation must not be a victim of what you are doing now.

King David understood that he was guilty of blood. He asked for God to deliver him.

Deliver me from blood guiltiness, O God, thou God of my salvation: *and* my tongue shall sing aloud of thy righteousness. Psalm 51:14 KJV

Many of the challenges we face or we're facing are from covenants in our past. No matter how you chase them and cast them out, as long as you don't use the word of God and the authority in the name of Jesus Christ, they won't go away.

Have you ever travelled to any country? If you have all the documents, there's no police or immigration personnel that will disturb or arrest you, why? Because you entered into that country legally. This is the same way our parents have given the enemy legal right to control us. Some of our parents were ignorant, some were aware of what they were doing and they still did it because they did not know the consequences the next generation will face.

The universe still exists not because of technology but because of Elohim's faithfulness to His word. The faithfulness of the word of the Creator is unexplainable and beyond understanding, only the Holy Spirit can reveal it to us.

It is only Elohim's word that has the capacity to transform and to save. On earth, much knowledge abounds but none of them is able to give eternal life except the knowledge of Yahweh that is able to transform and to save.

For the salvation of the world Elohim only sent His word.

**The greatest place of security is not in heaven nor on earth, but in God's word.**

**The spiritual and physical realm is controlled by the word of God.**

**Where Yahweh's word is, there is total protection.**

**We must be doers of the word to experience this energy. for us to function properly we need the energy that is in the word of God.**

**The vision of God is in His word, and living outside of the vision of God is rebellion, Yahweh spoke to prophet Ezekiel by calling the people of Israel a**

rebellious people because they didn't do His word.

We are the vision of God, through his word and his vision gives us life.

If the vision of your life is not aligned with the word of God, it will ruin and damage the essences of your existence. Understanding of this truth will secure your future.

## BREATH AND SOUND

### Breath

The air we breathe determines if we are still alive or dead. Why do doctors give oxygen to their patients? Because he or she cannot breathe by themselves. Even when God formed man with mud, he was not a living being until the breath of God came on him.

It is this breath that determines if we're alive or dead. Living to God means dead to the enemy and dead to the enemy means living to God.

Your actions determine who you honour as your source. You cannot serve two masters at once. If you serve two masters, you are owned by none.

I pray that you shall not live your life for nothing but you shall live your life for something.

The energy you catch from your inside determines the kind of energy you release. Can something that is dead give life? It's only the living who can give life. That's why the angels who appeared to Mary and the other said 'why are you looking for the living among the dead'?

While Jesus was in the spirit, He was alive but while He was in the flesh, he was dead. I'm telling you that dying to sin equals eternal life. Jesus could not die, because He was a sinless man who conquered sin.

**Prayer declaration**

Father in heaven, help me to benefit from your energy. I reject any negative voice producing negativity in me. In Jesus Christ name, Amen!

**Sound**

The sound effects in our environment are determined by the vessels releasing words over it. The kind of word released determines the wave of sounds that are produced. Positively or negatively.

The sound that accompanies our words describes a part of our natural body, the state of our soul, and the capacity of our spirit.

There's nature in the body, there's nature in the spirit, and there's also nature in the soul of men. Nature describes the uniqueness of each human on earth.

## Prayer declaration

Heavenly Father, I thank you, I pray that your word creates an enabling environment for me.

Give me the grace to live by your word, I speak life over all that concerns me.

The presences of the Holy Spirit will flood my space.

I revise any evil word spoken over my life by me or anybody else.

I stand in agreement with the word of God and I decree new seasons to start in my life and my family.

ABOUT THE AUTHOR

Founder of the Holy Ghost Kingdom Ministries International. He has a qualification in Supply Chain Management and Project Management, also in Computer Science. I encountered my calling at age of 11 and in 2008 the calling began to manifest by the power of deliverance. In 2013, I had a vision where this book is a part of it. It was

5am in the morning, while I was a permanent worker in one of the mining companies. My shift changed every 15 days starting from 3pm till the next day, and in the morning from 7am to 3pm. During one of my evening shifts, I went to the mountain as was my habit of having morning prayers by 5am until 12pm. When I left the mountain, I returned home to prepare for work. On getting home, I was so tired that I decided to rest. While resting, my eyes opened immediately and I found myself in front of the tabernacle of Moses. Curiously, when I looked inside the door, I saw a man sitting on a throne with a long white beard but I could not see the face only the beards and crown, and He asked me to come in. When I took the first step, I realized I was in front of Him and He told me to kneel which I did. Then He took the anointing oil, poured it on me and told me to go.

When I stood, I noticed there were two persons beside me, I checked and it was Aaron and Moses. After I left the tabernacle, I found myself in a big hall preaching to empty chairs but holding a hammer as a microphone. It took a while to understand this vision, up until I started serving, I doubted if I was indeed called by Elohim. After my night prayer session, the Lord opened my eyes again and I saw many people in a very dark place and they didn't know how to get out of it. Later, I saw a big board with a verse from Exodus rising from above. At that moment, I heard a voice speaking to me about the mission Yahweh gave me and the significant of the hammer I was holding as a microphone, this book is from my encounter years ago. I have many things to say in this book, continue reading. Your life is about to change for good. It took me 3 years to write this book and I understood why the enemy didn't want this book to be released.

www.ingramcontent.com/pod-product-compliance
Lightning Source LLC
Chambersburg PA
CBHW050841160426
43192CB00011B/2107